CONTENTS

SECTION 1

1334

F4V4M

TABLE OF CONTENTS

Page

Chapter I

CHANGES IN RECENT YEARS IN THE SCHOOL CURRICULUM.

Almost no other country hae passed through so many stages of development and in so short a time as the United States. The need of solving problems which required industrial knowledge, business skill, executive capacity, and personal efficiency arose. Where were people possessing these qualities to be found? Did the schools give the necessary training?

The first half century of our national life was a pioneer period- a period of great privation- a life of toil. Experience was the teacher and taught the people to make a living under the most exacting conditions. The boy worked by his father's side and learned to make and repair buildings, to make furniture for the home, to make the necessary farm implements, to care for the stock, and to supply all the raw materials required to sustain life. The girl received her education from her mother and grandmother. The skill she attained was due to constant participation in household duties.

In these early days, the family represented an independent unit- the farm and garden plots supplying all the raw material that was needed and the home transforming these into usable forms. All common articles like clothing, furniture, soap, smoked meats, butter, lard, etc. were made in the home. When larger tasks were to be done, there was an interchange of services in the neighborhood in some form similar to the husking bees or quilting parties. Thia made the home the center of the social life and consequently a strong home tie developed between the various members of the household.

Economic and social changes have crept in to alter these conditions. With the introduction of steam, electricity, and machinery, old occupations and methods gave way to the new. The race was relieved of the constant and pressing struggle for existence. Inventions such as the threshing machine, the reaper, and the sewing machine changed the whole aspect of life. With the increase in immigration the character of the people changed. From the north of Europe came a class of people who were intelligent, who could adapt themselves easily and quickly to the existing conditions and who possessed those characteristics which were essential for the new settler namely, self reliance and initiative. From the south came those who tended to corrupt civil life. They settled in groups in different sections of the northern states, spoke their own language, and made no attempt to become Americans. This increase in population and the gathering of people into towns led to a specialization of labor and the centralization of power into a few hands. The factory system developed. Class distinction became apparent. The home was no longer the work shop. Nearly all industries were carried on outside the home. Food was partly prepared for consumption and clothing and house furnishings were largely made in the factories. What little work that was left to be done in the home was made easier by the labor saving devices. Was it to be marvelled at that with the reduction of woman's work in the home and the increase of leisure time, that she enlarged her sphere and spent her efforts in serving her community, town, or country as well as her home. Has education kept pace with these changes?

2

SECTION 2

In the early period, the need for an education was small. To illiterate was no disgrace. Not until after 1S37 when Horace Mann inaugurated an educational revival in Massachusetts did the people begin to consider imposing a tax so that all might have an equal opportunity along educational lines. By 1S50, tax supported schools were generally accepted in the north and by the end of the civil war in the south.

Reading, writing, and arithmetic constituted the course of study. Later history, grammar, and geography were added. There was no grading of children. The term was short. The teacher was poorly trained. The method of instruction used was almost entirely individual. As soon as the child felt that he knew his lesson, he went forward and recited it to the teacher. Only those children who worked well alone succeeded. The others soon became discouraged and withdrew from school.

In the period from 1875 to 1900, practical men took the school to task and asked that the school concentrate its efforts toward a more definite purpose and train for a more useful life.

Many questioned the advisability of giving to the school the task of fitting a particular person for a particular job. Practical work was not considered cultural. It did not take long, however, to show that the practical subjects not only taught people how to earn a living but also how to live and therefore developed character.

Educators as well as the men of the practical field saw that the school was not meeting the needs of the people and that many of the pupils remained in school because the law required them to be there and not because they enjoyed the work. They pur- sued a course which neither they nor their parents could see any value in and then at about the age of fourteen they began their career with the hope that somehow the tide of opportunity would carry them to some safe destination.

One of the most intensive studies of conditions under which children left school in this country to go to work is to be found in one of the volumes on Woman and Child Wage Earners in the United States published by the United States Government in 1910. This investigation showed that of the six hundred and twenty-two (622) children studied who had left school:

30 percent had to aid in support of the family or self.

27 " because help was desired but not necessary.

26.6 "of child's dissatisfaction with school.

5.7 " " " ill health, to learn a trade, and

other minor excuses.

9.8 " because child preferred to work.

This showed that two thirdaof the children who dropped out of school for work could have remained. if they had been intelligently influenced and could have found it worth while to etay in school. The proportion of girls forced by financial circumstances to leave school was comparatively small. Being backward in their grades, dislike of school, desire for a change, and desire to be with friends who were working were their principal reasons.

The report of the commission appointed by the governor of Massachusetts also showed that children left school because neither they nor their parents could see any practical value in remaining there, but that a large majority of the parents could afford to keep their children in school for a year or two longer

and would do eo if they had an opportunity of securing a training which would make for industrial efficiency.

From the above mentioned investigations and others which were carried on, the most important reason unearthed for the children leaving school was that the parents realized that, at the end of each successive grade, their children were in no better position to enter upon an industrial career than before. One curriculum was formed for the children of all people and that course of study prepared pupils to meet the next higher grade, school or college. If the pupils did not care or respond to the uniform course, they were made to feel that their place was not in school.

In a democratic country like the United States the course of study had to expand in order to meet the present day demands caused by the social and economic changes. Investigation simply emphasized the fact that in order to retain a large percent of the children in school for a longer period than even before a broader and richer curriculum had to be introduced. Instruction had to be given which would coordinate the school work with the environment of the pupils. To meet these requirements vocational education, commerce, agriculture, manual training and home economics was installed in the majority of the schools in this country.

Vocational education was not new. Formerly practically all education was vocational. When learning was confined to the clergy, men were trained for the church. In Athene, citizens were trained for the performance of the duties of citizenship. The Romans were trained in law. During the middle ages, universities were established for the purpose of studying law, medicine, and theology. Training along other lines was not necessary. However, in order to meet the coraplexing problems of the present day, the new vocations had to be taught.

To see that training in home economics was as essential as training in agriculture or manual training has taken a long time. Many failed to realize that

(1) Sooner or later the majority of the girls would be engaged' in the activities connected with home making.

(2) The teaching of home economics would help to dignify the work of the home. This was necessary because apparently there were greater attractions in positions and wages outside of the home than in the home. Work in offices, factories, and stores received first consideration and few there were who would take up the work in the home.

(3) The greatly extended opportunity for girls and women to earn a livelihood in industry has decreased the amount of hired help available and consequently increased need for efficiency in the work of the home.

(U-) The secondary schools made such demands that the training in the hone has been curtailed.

(5) On account of the mother and daughter being separated the greater part of the day, the traditional method of transmitting from mother to daughter was inadequate and conaequently the school had to do its part in training these young girls to be the mothers and homemakers of the future.

(6) The taking of the preparation of many articles of food and the making of garments outside of the home has made training in home economics a necessity in order for the young housewife to be economical and know what to buy.

(7) The crowded living conditions have emphasized the importance of modern scientific knowledge of sanitation and hygiene.

Home economics certainly helped many girls to establish right standards of utilization and consumption and effective powers of working. What can the one branch of home economics namely, clothing and textiles do for the girl of today?

This branch is just beginning to receive the attention due it. More people are coming to realize every day that

(1) Since the cost of clothing is advancing at such a rapid rate, it is necessary for the young women to either make their own garments or at least be able to make the bought garment wear longer.

(2) Since the material in the ready made garment is inferior to the yard goods, it denotes greater thrift to spend what money ia available in purchasing good material rather than in paying for a style which will soon be out of vogue.

(3) By being well dressed, a woman can convince her associates and co-workers of her strong womanly qualities and she will have the right influence upon the production of the textile fabrics and welfare of the garment makers.

(U-) By having a knowledge of textiles as related to clothing and the development of skill in their uses, a correct feeling toward the beautiful and an appreciation of what is good taste in dress is created. This helps to put a stamp of disapproval on the absurd creations seen on the streets of today.

Lessons like these lead to greater efficiency in both the economic and social fields.

3

SECTION 3

Chapter II

THE GREAT PROBLEM.

The greatest problem which the home economics teacher has to face is that of correlating the work in the school with the home and community. The demand for home economics came from the home and the community and therefore it is no more than fair that the school should meet their needs. The time is now ripe because there is always a greater need for service Just after a great war than at any other time.

If the teacher is new in the community, ehe should make a survey in order to determine what the needs are. To do this, it may be wise for the teacher to have a conference with the principal and parents in order to obtain some clearly defined ideas. The teacher may even appoint committees among the girls to help her solve this problem.

The following concrete suggestions may prove to be of some help to the teacher in discovering what the existing organizations are that she may utilize- the teacher bearing in mind that the education of the community is as important a feature in her work as the education of the girls.

1- Is there a parent teachers association in your community? If so, are its members acquainted with the work done by the home economics department? If not, could the teacher organize a club amoung the mothers? This was worked out very successfully in one community. At the beginning of the year, the teacher sent out an invitation to all mothers of the school asking them to come to a tea and demonstration given by the girls in the clothing department on a certain day. About thirty mothers appeared. The teacher

gave a very helpful illustrated talk on "Short Cute in Sewing"

assisted a few of her pupils. Then the other girls served tea and wafers and acted as hostesses in escorting the mothers around the building. On this occasion the teacher asked if the mothers would like to meet frequently for such meetings and of course practically every one was willing and anxious. Arrangements were completed for regular meetings every two weeks and a small charge of five cents was made to pay for the supplies the girls used in preparing the refreshments. The club increased in attendance and the support the teacher received from these mothers was marvelous. Before the year was over, they had made garments for some of the school children who were in great need besides receiving many valuable suggestions for their own home sewing. A committee was appointed at the close of school year to arrange for reorganizing the club the following September. When this teacher was asked whether or not she had been repaid for her extra effort, she replied, "Oh, Yes. Mothers realize that their daughters can get something that is of real value in the school and consequently they cooperate with me and give me all the suggestions possible for the success of this work. Why the whole community knows about us and are interested in us."

2- The day nursery attracts the attention of the growing girl. It may be possible to arrange a trip so that the school girls can visit the day nursery and actually see what is being done for the little unfortunates who are left with but few of the advantages offered in this life. An experience of this kind will make a deep impression on the young mind and the teacher will find them vastly more interested in their clothing work than ever before.

3- Interest requires no stimulus in the class which a- dopts a war orphan. The teacher can secure information as to the kind of help that the class may render by writing to the Committee for Fatherless Children of France, 665 Fifth Avenue, New York City, or to the Committee for Armenian Relief, 1 Madison Avenue, New York City.

U>- Perhaps the associated charities are located in your community. They always have on their lists families that need help. One teacher, through this organization, found a group of seven widows who had forty-two children among them to feed and clothe. Can teachers imagine the happiness that came into these homes when blouses, dresses, and other garments were sent in for the wee tots. Cases similar to these exist in nearly every community. For work of this kind the associated charities will usually furnish the necessary materials.

5- Then there is the home service branch of the Red Cross. It also has many families on its lists which it is helping to raise the standard of living and would only be too glad to give its cooperation to the teacher in order to get the girls started in the social service work.

6- The group which receives the mother's pension needs help. The small pitance which these mothers receive does not begin to clothe and feed the children. The mother is forced to work. Will she not appreciate a deed of kindness?

7- Is there a Friendship Club in the community? These clubs were originally started in Washington, D. C. by high school girls, but the results of their work were so telling that now they have spread all over the country. In the cities, the Friendship

Clubs are usually connected with the Young Woman's Christian Association and have as their main object the helping of others. Could not one be organized in the high school in the smaller towns where the Y W A has not yet been established.

8- The girls of the home economics department may also

be the ones to distribute the government bulletins to the interested women of the community.

9- In still other places, "Neighborhood Houses" are to be found or there are "Girl Scouts" or "Camp Fire Groupe".

Many times a girl can be interested in doing for others and really made to enjoy rendering a service but dislikes doing the same thing at home. All girls pass through this stage and the wise teachers and mothers will make good use of it. Is it not worth while to interest girls in those things which certainly touch life and enable the girls to see their relationship to some of its problems.

A grave danger may arise among the enthusiastic teachers and that is the establishing of so many lines of interest that a lack of thoroughness results. This means weakness. In beginning this kind of work remember the old adage, "One thing done and that done well is a very good thing we all can tell!

By connecting the community interests and the instructive interests of the girl as suggested in the following chapter, a well rounded course can be planned and the girl be given a fair and accurate knowledge of how she may be of service in the home and a helpful factor in the community.

Chapter III
A SUGGESTIVE PLAN FOR THE
TEACHING OF CLOTHING AND TEXTILES.

During the past few years, the method of teaching which has been gaining in favor in all subjects is that known as the project and problem plan. By the project and problem plan is meant the organization of material around some activity that is to be accomplished by the solving of many problems. In other words, the project is an act carried to completion and in so doing involves the solution of problems.

For example, a teacher is meeting her class which is ready to start a new garment. Nothing has been said to the class about it. The teacher opens the lesson by saying, "Our problem of making the kimona aprons is completed and at the close of this lesson I am going to give you an opportunity to grade them. In the meantime, I want you to decide on what you want to make next. I have secured several pieces of simple underwear and dresses from the stores for you to look at and perhaps these will help you in making your decision. However, before you make your decision, what is the one question you must keep in mind?"

Member of class, "What garments can I make in school that I need?"

This thought has been emphasized by the teacher throughout the year and really becomes the big project.

Teacher, "Grace, will you make a list on the blackboard of the garments the girls would like to make?"

Grace steps to the board and writes names of articles as they are suggested by the pupils.

Discussion begins. Ruth objects to making a dress because

it is too hard and would take too long. Agnes does not want to make a waist and skirt because girls of her age wear only one piece dresses. Hazel says that her mother would like to have her make a pair of bloomers.

Teacher, "Would it not be wise for you to have Grace also make a list of the different problems that you have had in sewing?"

This helps the girls to see that they must choose a simple problem. The decision is finally in favor of making the bloomers. The teacher's suggestions lead up to the decision but the girls feel that they themselves have selected the next garment to be made.

Now the girls see their project as a whole, the making of a useful garment namely, bloomers, and the next step is the solving of problems that will arise such as, "Shall I draft or use a commercial pattern?", "What kind of material shall I buy?", "How many yards shall I buy?", "What kind of seams shall I use?", "What kind of a finish or trimming will give the best service?" and so on ad infinitum. It is surprising how many and how fast the questions will arise.

There are many advantages in using a method of this kind.

(1) The children have planned their own work and consequently will be more interested in it. This is only human nature. Children rebel when told to do a thing, but, if they can be made to feel that they had a part in its planning, they will enter into it with all their heart and soul and see the act carried through to completion.

(2) A definite goal to be reached is defined. Every pupil realizes that she has a certain garment to make and probably within a set time.

4

SECTION 4

(3) The subject *i3*presented as a whole and thus definite reasons can be seen for talcing up certain steps at various lessons. This gives a real reason for the teaching of very lesson and unity in the work.

A method of this kind also has its limitations. Unless the teacher is a wise and allseeing guide the pupils are apt to make what they like rather than what they need. The teacher must ask herself whether or not the children are selecting that which will be of real educational value in the way of presenting new problems or whether the garment is simply a repetition of the old. A list of problems and accomplishments should be kept so that the teacher can make an inventory or take stock every now and then and determine whether or not the necessary problems are being included in the years work.

The teacher then has a two-fold duty (1) guide the children in making their choices and (2) see that the right subject matter is presented.

Before giving the suggestive course, a word should b written about the subject matter. One important note of warning is that it should be kept up to date. This can be done by the teacher attending teachers institutes, conventions, and association meetings, reading journals and publications of the government and other sources, attending summer schools at different universities, attending lectures when possible, and making visits to factories and stores to find out the latest ways of finishing garments and the short cuts that are used.

With the subject matter well in hand the following course may be of value in helping the teacher to see what projects may

arise, what the problems are that are apt to develop and what illustrative material may be used in making the lessons clear.

This course may be given in the junior or senior high schools. It requires no scientific background nor any previous training in sewing. Best results can be obtained if the clase meets for one hour each day and is required to do some home work. However this course may be made to fit into any school program.

Garments are listed in the order usually taken in the teaching of clothing and textiles. However, this order may be changed as the teacher sees fit. For example, the girls may decide to make a petticoat first. This is just as good as a work apron because the first problem is really used to give practice on the use of the sewing machine. Other garments than those listed may be selected so long as they are not too difficult for the pupil, are of educational value, and present the lessons which the teacher feels are important for the girls to have.

5

SECTION 5

The above course of study is only suggestive. No definite course can be made out which will fit conditions in every school. For example, a course suitable for a large city high school could not be adopted by the school in a small village. This is true partly because, in the latter, equipment is limited, library facilities are lacking, and the teacher can not give all of her time in planning work for one subject. The general outline will possibly be the same but fewer side tracks or inroads into the subject can be made. Much, so far as related subjects are concerned, will depend on the knowledge and practical experience of the teacher. What are some of the related subjects that could be handled in the average school?

There are few teachers who do not recognize the importance of a lesson on clean hands. Many children do not know what the term "clean hands" really means. Time can be well spent by the teacher in giving a simple demonstration in manicuring and then allowing the children to practice on one another.

Another lesson may be that of care of clothing in school and at home. How many girls have been taught the use of shoe trees or to dust their shoes at night, or to brush and hang up their clothes instead of throwing them on the floor, or to mend their clothes as soon as a rip appears, or to clean garments at regular intervals and not to wait until the garments are so covered with spots that it takes half a day to renovate them.

This lesson may be closely linked with the subject of dyeing because often the only way to renovate a dress is to change its color. This may also include removal of stains, pressing

various kinds of material and garments, and even laundering.

The subject of appropriate color combinations may be made a most interesting and profitable lesson by having the girls select appropriate designs for various occasions from fashion sheets, trace, and then color, using complimentary, analagous, or contrasting color schemes. One design may be chosen and worked out in the various color schemes so that the girl may see the results for herself.

Still another lesson of value is that on the use of the sewing machine attachments. The majority of the homes today can boast of a sewing machine but very few women are able to use the attachments. Many are the short cuts that can be made if the mothers only know how. There are not enough demonstrators in the country to act as teachers but the daughter can be a real help in carrying the lesson home from the school.

Lessons on mending can be brought in whenever the teacher sees fit. Too often the interest in this subject lags because the children know that every other Tuesday is reserved for mending. This difficulty though may be easily overcome by the teacher working in a lesson now and then as the opportunity presents itself. If, for example, a project such as the making of a middy blouse or a skirt requires a long time, the children grow tired of it. Let them put it aside for one or two lessons and do some mending for their mothers. Their interest will be revived in the old project and they will accomplish a great deal more than if they had continued on the old problem.

Another topic which is of vital interest and which should be introduced in the first year and carried on through the

second is that of the keeping of budgets. 3y taking inventory of clothing on hand and keeping track of the cost of garments for a definite period the girls begin to realize what clothes cost and it may lead to them taking better care of their clothes. It will also help them to apportion their money, when they begin to work, so that they will not have to buy their expensive garments on the installment plan. Catastrophies such as having the garments taken away by the merchants or their pay garnisheed or their credit lost in a community will be avoided. Emphasis need not be placed upon clothing only but practice may be given in the making out of suggestive budgets which would include all needs and cultural wants and thus the value of conservation and thrift made clear.

Of even greater or at least equal value to budgets ie that of caring for the baby. This does not include the food and its preparation because that comes in the food course. Every girl should be able to dress and bathe a baby easily and quickly. If a real baby can be obtained for demonstrational work, so much the better. The girls may even want to adopt a baby and care for it during the day and then return it to the mother at night. A project of this kind can easily be worked out especially if there is not a day nursery in the town or city. There are many mothers who would be willing to have their babies taken care of at the school under the supervision of the teacher. In this case layettes can be made for the adopted babies.

Many interesting problems can be brought out in the school in connection with ready made versus home made garments. The girls may work out certain problems and draw their own conclusions as to whether or not it shows greater thrift and industry

on their part to 'make their clothes rather than to buy them. One girl may test out the wearing quality of a bought night gown in comparison to the one she may make in school. Different girls in the class may take different problems and thus every one be able

to enter into a real live discussion at the end. At this discussion, it would be well to have ready to wear garments and garments which the girls have made on hand so that the girls could really see why the bought garments gave less service than the garments made at home or in school. There are some garments like shoes and stockings that are always purchased. Girls may work on problems of extending the length of service of these articles. For example, a girl may test out the wearing qualities of hose by taking three pairs and wearing one the ordinary way, that is wear until soiled and then wash and darn and use again. The second is washed out every night and darned whenever necessary. The third, before being worn, is strengthened by putting in running stitches with darning cotton in toe, heel, and any other place that wears out quickly and then the pair is rinsed out every night. It is not necessary to state what the results will be. In this way every problem will have a definite plan of procedure and lead up to some discussion which will clinch the lesson that the teacher has been trying to drive home.

Contests in recognizing weaves and materials will create fun as well as be of an educational value.

The teacher can see from the list of subjects suggested that a course in clothing and textiles does not include only the construction of garments. There are so many interesting topics that the danger arises here similar to the one in correlating the

work of the home, school, and community. A few subjects well chosen so as to fit the needs of the girls in the particular community and well taught will give the best satisfaction in the end.

Chapter IV

ILLUSTRATIVE MATERIAL.

One of the difficulties found in the teaching of clothing is that of the teacher being unable to present facts clearly so that every member of the class may understand them. There are many children to whom explanation by word of mouth means very little but to whom some illustrative material may be of greatest value in helping them to visualize the lesson.

This does not necessarily mean that the teacher must have innumerable objects on hand which she can present at a moment's notice. But, in the first place, she must give some thought to the choice of the material and only produce that which will enrich and strengthen the lesson. Finished garments may be shown so that the pupils may receive a definite idea as to what their finished products should be like. Large samples of various kinds of material may be used in the study of weaves, kinds of fibers, adulterations used in the manufacture of textiles. Trips may be made to various places of interest instead of bringing material into the class room. Pictures and models may take the place of actual garments when it comes to the discussion of lines in dress, design, development of styles, etc. Or, if the teacher is at all gifted in drawing, she may be able to hold the interest of students by making rough sketches. The pupils may even make the illustrative material in the form of posters or garments such as a layette for the permanent school exhibit.

In the second place, the teacher must know how to use the illustrative material. Unless wisely used, it may as easily

mar as make the lesson. Pupils should be told what to look for in advance of the presentation of the article or demonstration. For example, if the teacher shows the burning test as a simple home test, which can be used to distinguish cotton from wool and silk, she should explain to the children first that cotton fibers burn rapidly while wool and silk fibers go out as soon as they are taken away from the flame and also give off a very disagreeable odor. Then the teacher may perform the test and the pupils will have a clear vision of it.

In the third place, the material must be timely. Try showing the pupils different styles of work aprons secured from the local stores when the problem is that of making a dress and see what the result is. In other words, the material introduced should, except in rare cases, apply directly to the lesson being taught.

In the fourth place, the illustrative material should be limited in amount. Too many articles lead to confusion. One good picture or article is worth a dozen mediocre ones.

In the fifth place, simplicity should dominate. Often, garments are brought in that are so attractive that the pupils become absorbed in the garment itself and miss the lesson entirely that the garment was supposed to illustrate. Elaborate garments may have their place but the teacher must know how to use them wisely. On the other hand, the garment must not be so simple that little effort is required to look at it. The pupils will glance at the object, think that they know all there is to know about it but fail when the final teat comes.

What is this final teat? In order that the teacher may feel certain that the pupils have gleaned all that is desirable it is well to have the pupils give back in some form or other such as in an oral recitation or a theme that which the pupil hae observed. This gives the pupil a chance to organize her thoughts and the teacher an opportunity to clear up any haziness or misunderstanding.

Materials Obtainable from Manufacturers. Silk:-

1- Corticelli Silk Mills, Florence, Mass.

(a) "Silk, Its Origin, Culture, and Manufacture."

Bound in green cloth-2-.

(b) Silk specimens mounted on cards, showing all of the

important steps in the manufacture including cocoons,

raw silk ready for spinning, twisting, etc.$0

set of eight cards. Postage6,

(c) Corticelli Silk Culture Cabinet $2.50. If purchased for a permanent school exhibit, $1.25.

2- The H. K. H. Silk Co. Inc., 120 E. l6th Street, New York

City.

(a) Small glass top exhibition box containing (l) chrysalis, (2) cocoon, (3) raw silk, (U) manufactured silk, (5) gum-boiled out, (6) spun silk, (7) sewing silk, (8) buttonhole twist, (9) dyed pure silk, (10) fiber silk, (11) pure embroidery floss, (12) Texto rope silk.

3- Cheney Brothers, Fourth Ave. and Eighteenth St., New York City.

(a) The Story of Silk.

(b) A Glossary of Silk Terras.

(c) A Short Description of Silk and Silk Manufacture.

(d) The Miracle Workers.

(e) Why do You call them Polka Dots.

(f) An exhibit is in preparation which when completed
will show the entire process of manufacture from
the cocoon to the finished product. Available about
Sept. 1, 1920.

U- Williaa Skinner and Sons, 305- 309 W. Adams, Cor. Frank-
lin Street, Chicago, 111.

(a) Silk and Satins, Their Romantic Story.

(b) Booklets containing samples of all silks.

5- National Ribbon Company, U-O Fourth Ave., New York City, (a) Pamphlet on process of weaving silk ribbons with
samples and illustrations. $1.00. Wool:-

1- International Harvester Co., 606 S. Michigan Ave.,
Chicago, 111.

(a) Bulletins on wool. Manila and Sisal Hemp:-

1- International Harvester Co., S. Michigan Ave.,
Chicago, 111.

(a) Booklet on hemp.

(b) "The Story of Twine".

(c) "Binder Twine Industry".

Cotton:-

1- The Spool Cotton Co., 315 Fourth Ave, Corner Twenty
Fourth St., New York City.

(a) Evolution of Cotton Thread.

(b) Spool Cotton Exhibits. Supply exhausted at present date, June 1, 1920, but expect to have a further supply in the near future.

Textilee:-

KnightMcKnight, Normal, Illinois.

Exhibitssilk, wool, flax, cotton, hemp, juteramie.$3-50each.

LudlowManufacturingAssociation, DevonshireSt.,
Boston, Mass.

(a) Exhibit of raw flax, jute, Italian and American
hemp; roving and yarn. $300.

3- Luther Ford and Company, Minneapolis, Minnesota.

(a) Home Laundry Hints.

- M. J. Whittall, Worcester, Maas.

(a) Booklet, Oriental Art in Whittall Rugs.

5- Mallineon's Silk Co., New York City.

(a) Booklet, Yesterday and Today. Weaving:-

1- L. S. Watson Manufacturing Co., Leicester, Mass.

(a) Heddles and heddle frames, (write for prices).

2- Thomas Charles Company, 229-53 Calumet Ave., Chicago, 111.

(a) Looms (write for kinds and prices).

Scissors:-

1- Thomas Charlea Company, 224-9-53 Calumet Ave., Chicago, 111.

(a) School Sciaaore (write for catalogue).   Bulletins:- I- U. S. Department of Agriculture, Washington, D. .

1- Bureau of Publication.

No. 165, Silk Worm Culture.

No. 274-, Flax Culture.

No. 29, Leaeona on Cotton for the Rural Common Schools.

No. 669, Fiber Flax.

No. 787, Sea Island Cotton.

No. 86l, Removal of Stains from Clothing and other Textiles.

2- Bureau of Plant Industry, Washington, D. C.

Circular 28, The Strenth of Textile Plant Fibers. " 103, Ramie.

3- Bureau of Animal Industry, Washington, D. C.

No. 322, Utilization of American Flax Straw in the Paper and Fiber Board Industry.

Circular 81, The Sheep Industry of England, Scotland, Ireland, and France.

- Office of Experiment Stations, Washington, D. C.

No. 33, The Cotton Plant, 60.

5- Bureau of Entomology, Washington, D. C.

Circular 36, The True Clothes Moth.

6- States Relation Service, Office of Extension Work, North and West, Washington, D. C.

W. S. Ill, 12, Conservation of Clothing.

W. S. V, g, Part I and II, Home Care of Clothing.-

W. S. V., 9, Good Buying.

Farmers Bulletin 1089- Selection and Care of Clothing.

Thrift Leaflet No. 5- Easier Laundry Methods.

"' " " 6- How to Remove Stains.

"' " " 7- Taking Care of Your Clothing.

"' " " S- Special Cleaning.

7- Federal Board for Vocational Education, Washington, Bulletin No. 23 (Home Economics Series, No. 1), Clothing for the Family.

8- United States Tariff Commission, Washington, D. C.

Tariff Information Series, No. 3, Schedule L. Silk and Manufacturers of Silk, 191S.
II- Department of Commerce and Labor.
1- Bureau of Agriculture, Manila, P. I.
Farmers Bulletin No. 12, Abaca (Manila Hemp)
Bulletin No. 26, The Kapok Industry.
Circular No. 21, Kapok Culture.
Ill- State Institutions of Learning.
1- Extension Service of the College of Agriculture,
University of Wisconsin, Madison, Wisconsin.
Circular 65, Sewing for Girls.
113> Making Clothes Last Longer.
" 91, New Clothes at Small Cost.
2- Agriculture Extension Department, Iowa State College
of Agriculture and Mechanic Arts, Ames, Iowa.
Home Economics Bulletin, No. 4, Textiles- Their
Care and Use.
Home Economice Bulletin, No. 9, Planning the
Costume.
Emergency Leaflet, No. 51, Clothing Thrift.
Emergency Leaflet, No. 53, Short Cuts in Sewing.
3- Extension Service in Agriculture and Home Economics
of College of Agriculture, University of Illinois,
Urbana, Illinois.
Extension Circular, No. 35, Color in Dress.
" 3, Artistic Dress.
" 33, Fashion, Its Use and
Abuse.
Extension Circular, No. lSuggestion for Garment
Making.
1- Extension Division, Michigan Agricultural College,
East Lansing, Michigan.
Extension Course Notes, No. 20, Clothing for Children.
" " " "21, The Care of Clothing.
"' "' 22, How to Know Materials.
" " " 23, How to Buy Clothing.
" " "24-, Home Dress Making
Patterns.
Extension Course Notes, No. 25, Remodeling.
" " " 26, Layettes.
5- Agriculture Extension Division, University of Minne
sota, University Farm, St. Paul, Minn.
Special Bulletin, No. 15, Textiles.
" " " 25, Clothing Conservation
for Home and Community.
Extension Bulletin, No. 27, Flax Growing.

6- Agricultural College Extension Service, Ohio State
University, Columbus, Ohio.
Extension Bulletin, Vol. X No. 5 Textiles and Dress.
" " XII No. 9, Sewing.
" " No. 7 Home Laundering.
7- Department of Agricultural Extension, Purdue Univer
sity, LaFayette, Indiana.
Extension Bulletin No. 74– New Uses for Old Cloth-
ing.
Leaflet, No. 105, Textiles:- Problems in Buying,
Cleaning, and Dyeing.
8- Oregon Agricultural College Extension Service, Corval-
lis, Oregon.
Extension Bulletin, No. 188, Some Pointe in Choosing
Textiles.
Extension Bulletin, No. 227, Stitches, Seams and
Sewing Processes.
Extension Bulletin, No. 221, Clothing Conservation I.
"' "' " 222, " " II.
"' " " 223, " " HI,
9- Extension Division, University of Idaho, Boise, Idaho.
Extension Bulletin No. 13, First Year Sewing.
'" " 26, Clothing Selection for Women.
Extension Bulletin No. 27, Selection of Clothing
for Children.
10- Extension Service, North Dakota Agricultural College,
Fargo, North Dakota.
Circular No. 25, Selection and Care of Textiles.
" " 26, Helps for the Home Dressmaker.
11- College of Industrial Arts, Dentón, Texas.
Bulletin- How to Use, Care for, and Buy the Family
Wardrobe.
12- Department of Agricultural Extension, Pennsylvanie
State College, State College, Pennsylvania.
Circular 48- Childrens Clothing.
13- Extension Service, Rhode Island State College, King
ston, Rhode Island.
Bulletin, No. 5, Thrift in Clothing.
14– Bureau of Publications, Teachers College, Columbia
University, New York City.
No. 1- Economic Function of Woman- E. T. Devine- 100
" 4– Hints on Clothing- M. S. Woolman- 100.
"' 7- Determination of Linen and Cotton, Dr. Her-
zog, 25$.
No. 9- The Girl of Tomorrow- What the School Will

Do for Her, B. R. Andrews, 100.
15- Agricultural Extension Service, University of Nebraska,
Lincoln, Nebraska.
Circular 1, Comparison of Textile Fabrics.
Circular 3, Care of Clothing and Cleaning.
" 1, Suggestions for Designing Clothing.
" 5 Conservation of Clothing.
" 6, Sewing Equipment.
" 7, Alteration of Patterns.
" 8, Color Combinations in Clothing.
" 9 The Planning of a Economical Wardrobe.
" 10, Uses for Old Clothe.
"HomeMadeDressForm.

6

SECTION 6

BIBLIOGRAPHY.

Books:-

Bagley, W. C.- Educational Values- The MacMillan Co.-
New York City- 1911.

Baldt, Laura I.- Clothing for Women- J. B. Lippincott
Co.- Philadelphia- 1916.

Bloomfield, Meyer- Youth, School, and Vocation- Houghton
Mifflin Co.- New York City- 1915-

Colvin, S. S.- The Learning Process- MacMillan Co.-
New York City- 1912.

Colvin, S. S.- An Introduction to High School Teaching-
MacMillanYorkCity1919.

Cooley, AnnaDomesticWoman'sEducationCharlee
Scribner'sSonsYorkCity1911.

Cooley, Winchell, Spohr, MarshallTeachingHome
EconomicsMacMillanYorkCity
1919.

Cubberly,

ChangingConceptionEducationHoughton
MifflinYorkCity1909.
Dean, WorkerStateCentury
YorkCity1910.
Fales,
JaneDressmakingCharlesScribner'sSons
YorkCity1917.
Gillette,
VocationalEducationAmericanBook
YorkCity1910.
Inglis, Alex.
PrinciplesSecondaryEducationHoughton
MifflinYorkCity1919-
Kent, E. B.- Constructive Interests of Children- Thesie-
Columbia University- New York City- 1903.
Lapp and Mote- Learning to Earn- Bobbs, Merrill Co,-
Indianapolis, Indiana- 1916.
Leavitt, F. M.- Examples in Industrial Education.
Schmit, Celestino L.- Garments for Girls- The Century
Co.- Ne York City- 1919.
Snedden, D. S.- The Problem of Vocational Education-
Hough ton Liifflin Co.- New York City- 1910.
Snedden, D. S.- Vocational Homemaking Education- Houghton
Mifflin Co.- New York City- 1912.
Van Renasalaer, Rose, and Canon- Manual of Homemaking-
The MacMillan Co.- New York City- 1919.
Wilson, H. B. and Wilson, G. M.- The Motivation of School
Work- Houghton Mifflin Co.- New York City.
Teacher's Collage Records:-
Xilpatrick- The Project Method- ¿918.
Xilpatrick and Others- Horace Mann Studies- 1916.
Van Hofe- Development of a Project- 1916.
Winchell, Cora- Planning the Leseon- 1915.
Bullet ins:-
Clothing for the Family- Federal Board for Vocational Edu-
cation- Washington, D. C.
Survey of Needs in Field of Vocational Home Economics Edu-
cation- Federal Board of Vocational Education-
Washington, D. C.
Course of Study for High Schools- Kansas State Board of
Education- Topeka, Kansas.
Three Short Courses in Komemaking- Carrie Lyford.
Speyer System- Teachers' College- New York City.
Suggestions for the Teaching of Home Economics in High
Schools of Mississippi- Supt. of Public

Education- Jackson, Miss.
Journals:-
Journal of Home Economics- March, 1920.
" " "' April, 1920.
APPROVED:-
1405557
9982557a

Lightning Source UK Ltd.
Milton Keynes UK
172951UK00002B/193/P